MINEC

DIARY OF A MINECRAFT PIG

Steve Miner

TABLE OF CONTENTS

Entry One

Hello, my name is Pinky, the Pig. I live in Minecraft with my owner. The rest of the Minecrafters call him Steve, but I prefer calling him Boss.

Well, my Boss took me in when I was still a small pig. You see, I was naughty little fella' and kept running away from my mum.

One day, I wandered away into the

wood and got lost. As the night fell, I did not know the way back to my mummy.

So I started running around and calling for help. The wolves came and I think, they wanted to eat me.

Mum told me later that they just wanted to play, but I think she only said that to make me feel better.

Well, my Boss showed up from nowhere and saved me. I will always remember that moment when he took out his diamond sword, swung it high up in the air and ran towards the wolves. He was my hero.

Later, he picked me up, stroked me and even asked me if I was alright. Well, as you might guess – since then he is my best buddy.

I follow him around wherever he goes.

Entry Two

The villagers are making fun of poor Boss again. I have grown up in the main time and I try to defend my best friend, but he just tells me to stand still.

They called my Boss useless and they told him to never come back to the mines again.

I am very sad. My Boss has been sitting in his house for days, he won't speak to me or go outside at all.

I think the villagers have made him feel this way. I wish I could help him somehow...

Entry Three

I have had enough of this. I have to do something. I left Boss at the house, I even brought him some food and water, I really hope he will eat it, he looks so thin.

I went over to the mines, to find all those who have made him sad and tell me to apologize.

But, I am not sure how to tell them, they don't understand my language. But I understand theirs.

The miners saw me and laughed at me, saying that Boss got abandoned even by his stupid pig pet.

That made me angry, but I knew that Boss would not want me to fight or be aggressive, so I let them be. I spent days and nights at the mine.

I waited, I did not know for what I was actually waiting, but my pig instincts told me to be patient.

Entry Four

The day I was waiting had finally come. I heard the miners talking. Well, it is like they were whispering.

They were mentioning some magical red stone. I don't really know what that is, but I heard them say that the one who found that stone, would be the hero of the village.

I stayed there for a little longer and they mentioned the stone could only be found deep in the Nether and that the mines will be closing soon, if somebody doesn't find it soon.

I did not listen longer to their talking and ran off to my house.

While I was running, I heard them talking about some danger and something evil, but I couldn't wait any longer.

Entry Five

As soon as I got into the house, I saw my Boss. But, he was not alone in the house. He was talking to Carla, his childhood friend.

She was making some weird and funny faces and telling him jokes and Boss seemed to feel better. He was laughing.

My mum called this love, but I have never been in love, so I am not sure what that is like.

Boss didn't notice me, until I ran over to the table where he kept his potions and the equipment he always wore with himself in a small bag. I grabbed the bag and ran outside.

I heard my Boss saying to Carla "Look, even my pig thinks I am useless and he ran off now".

I could not explain anything more to Boss and decided I had to save him, like he saved me once a long time ago.

Entry Six

I have never been so far away from my home. I admit that I was a little bit scared. I met a few dogs on my way, asking them for directions.

They told me that the Nether is a dangerous place and that a pig will never survive there.

I did not mind their talk, I was determined to find this red stone, bring it back to the village and then my Boss is going to be a hero.

The villagers will see what a great miner he is and maybe even Carla will love him more.

The night was falling and I felt my tiny legs shivering. I think Boss said this meant that I was scared...

Entry Seven

I was already deep inside the forest, it seemed like I was walking for day.

I was not sure which way to go, so I just keep walking straight forward. Suddenly, I saw a huge Fortress in front of me.

That must be it, they are hiding the red stone right there. I was sure of that, so I excitedly ran towards it. But, before I got close to it, I was surrounded.

There were Wither Skeletons all around me, they were coming closer and one of them grabbed me.

I don't remember what happened after that, but I woke up tied up in ropes.

The Skeletons were sitting by a bonfire and talking to each other, but I didn't understand their language.

One of them came over to me. His eyes were so scary and he had long claws that were moving towards me.

" I am sorry Boss. I did not make it. I am going to die", I thought to myself and closed my eyes, hoping it would hurt less that way.

Entry Eight

When I opened my eyes there was nobody around me anymore. There was something like a gate in front of me, but I had never seen something like that. I think I was trapped.

Everything was dark and there was a weird smell. I tried opening that gate, but it seemed like it was locked.

I put my head through one of the holes and saw that these small cells were all around and there were animals in all of them: sheep, horses, cats, cows, chicken...

I did not know what was going on, but I think I was the only pig in there. I tried calling out to the other animals, but nobody wanted to talk to me.

Entry Nine

I did not know when there was night or day, but I think around 3 days passed since the Skeletons threw me into that small cell.

That day, one of the rabbits decided to talk to me. What he told me, made me both very happy and very frightened.

The rabbit, who called himself Fluffy,

told me that the Skeletons needed one animal of each species. I was the last part in their puzzle, as it was difficult to find pigs around Nether.

The reason that made me happy is that the rabbit mentioned the red stone.

Fluffy told me that the Skeletons had been planning to destroy the villagers for a long time already.

Their Witch told them they needed the red stone and that they had to sacrifice animals as a tribute to the monster they were about to summon.

This meant they would also kill Boss. I had to do something. Luckily, I remembered the bag I took from the house and I know that there some TNT inside as well.

I placed the TNT on the ground and soon after, it exploded. The cell door opened and I ran outside.

I could not leave the other animals behind, so I helped them get out as well. Now, all I needed was the red stone.

Entry Ten

I walked slowly into the main part of the Fortress. I could smell the Skeletons all around, but I wasn't scared anymore.

All I needed was the red stone and when I found it, I would run back to Boss and everything will be like it used to be.

I heard the Skeletons talking somewhere, but it all sounded just like odd noises to me. Suddenly, I saw Fluffy standing next to me.

He told me that he couldn't just leave me behind, after I saved him. He also told me what the Skeletons were saying :

"They are attacking the village tonight. The Witch wants to summon the monster with the red stone. But, they haven't noticed that we are gone yet, so we still have a chance".

We searched all around the castle, but we couldn't find the stone anywhere.

Entry Eleven

The sky seemed to be painting in a crimson color. The Skeletons were moving toward the village. We saw the witch going downstairs towards the dungeons.

I looked up through the window and saw an unusual glow coming from the rooftop. Fluffy and I ran upstairs and my idea turned out to be right.

In the middle of the roof we finally saw it. It was the magic red stones, with a giant circle drawn around it. It seemed like the ritual was supposed to happen right there.

But, I did not want to find out and wait for the Witch to come back, so I grabbed the stone and put it into my bag.

Fluffy and I were soon in the forest, running towards the village.

As soon as we leave Nether, the stone will belong to the villagers and the Witch cannot have it, ever again.

Entry Twelve

I could already see the gates, the boundary between the monsters and the villagers. We were almost there, just a few more steps.

My ears got filled with sounds of howling. I remembered the first time I met Boss, and I remembered that exact same scary sound.

Wolves were moving towards us. This

time I knew it, they did not want to play with us. We were dinner to them.

Fluffy hid behind me and I could hear his teeth trembling. We almost made it, but we could not fight the wolves.

But, my Boss once told me that all good deeds come back to you when you need them the most.

We saw all of the animals, that I saved in the dungeon, running towards us.

The horses were fighting off the wolves and I remembered having a light potion in my beg. I asked Fluffy to take it and throw it at the wolves.

Boss told me that they run away from the light and so it really happened. The wolves were gone and we were saved.

Entry Thirteen

The village was on fire. The Minecrafters were fighting against the Skeletons, and my home looked like a battle field.

Soon, the Witch appeared and gave the Skeletons the sign to retreat. Without the red stone they could never win against us.

I saw Boss, he was with Carla, trying to protect her. I ran towards him as fast as I could and handed him the stone. I remember him looking at me for a while, not blinking, not speaking.

He just looked at me, searching for an explanation in my eyes. He knew I had done it for him and that I finally found a way to repay him for everything he had ever done for me.

Entry Fourteen

Boss was the hero of the village, everything came back to normal. The mines were working again and my best friend was the most popular miner.

Carla would come over visit us every day, I heard her say that she was in love with my Boss. I liked Carla, she always brought me cookies and she made Boss smile.

Well, as for me, I found out two

things.

First – wolves don't want to play with pigs, they want to eat them.

Second- I found out what love really means.

----------------------- The End -------- ---------------------

Printed in Great Britain
by Amazon.co.uk, Ltd.,
Marston Gate.